Your Go-to Sausage Cookbook

Incredible Sausage Recipes that would Make You Love Sausages More!!!

by Chloe Tucker

© 2021 Chloe Tucker All Rights Reserved.

License Notes

All rights reserved. This publication cannot be distributed, reproduced, recorded, photocopied, or transmitted. If you desire to share this content, you must seek prior permission from the author. Beware, the author will not be held responsible for your interpretation of this content. However, it is fair to say that the content written herein is accurate.

Table of Contents

Introduction 5

   Sausage Pasta 7

   Spicy Stuffed Chicken Thighs.. 9

   Noodle Napoli 11

   Sausage Cheese Balls 13

   Broccoli, Rabe and Sausage.. 15

   Sausage, Kale and White Bean Soup 17

   Burrata Stuffed Burger 19

   German Currywurst.. 21

   Beer Brats 23

   Sausage Barley Soup.. 25

   Jalapeno and Blue Cheese Burger 27

   Toscana Soup 29

   Italian Style Nachos 31

   German Spaghetti 33

   Divine Burger... 36

Pork and Pepper Stir Fry	38
Low Carb Cheddar Cheese and Beef Burger	41
German Style Kale and Sausage	43
Breakfast Sausage	45
Low Carb Blue Cheese Burger	47
Sausage and Red Cabbage	50
Cilantro and Pork Sausage	52
Pork and Sausage Fried Rice	55
Portobello Mushroom and Pizza Burger	58
Country Sausage Gravy	60
Boere Breyani	63
Tuscan Soup	65
Italian Sausage Soup	67
BBQ Nachos	69
Biography	71
An Author's Afterthought	72

Introduction

One of the gravest culinary mistakes that people make is stereotyping a particular dish for a particular mealtime. Sausages are one of the food ingredients that have been stereotyped for breakfast only.

That is wrong because breakfast is not the only meal that you can cook with sausages. There are a lot of meals that you can prepare with sausages, and they would come out just fine!

Talk about grains, vegetables, meats, etc., there is no food item that you cannot combine with sausages that you won't enjoy, but the question remains, "how best can you combine your sausages?"

This sausage recipe book is here to teach you different exciting ways that you can combine sausages with other food items to get fantabulous dishes!!

||||||||||||||||||||||||||||||||||||||||||||||||||||||||||||||||||||||||||||||||||||

Sausage Pasta

This is a unique and easy recipe that is perfect for a quick lunch or dinner.

Duration: 15 minutes

Serving Size: 6

List of Ingredients:

- Pasta- ¾ pound
- Olive oil- 1 tbsp.
- Italian sausage- 1 pound
- Chopped onion- 1
- Garlic cloves- 4
- Chicken broth- 14.5 ounces
- Basil- 1 tsp.
- Tomatoes- 15 ounces
- Chopped spinach- 10 ounces
- Parmesan cheese- ½ cup

Preparation:

Boil the pasta in salted water.

Fry the sausage and the onion in olive oil.

Now add in the garlic.

Now add in the chicken broth, basil and tomatoes.

Cook for a few minutes before adding in the spinach.

Add the boiled pasta to the mixture and mix.

Sprinkle over the parmesan cheese and then serve!

Spicy Stuffed Chicken Thighs

Full of flavor, chicken baked with tomatoes, onion and bell pepper and stuffed with Italian sausage, this recipe is a must try!

Duration: 15 minutes.

Serving Size: 5.

List of Ingredients:

- Chicken thighs- 10
- Italian sausages- 5
- Diced green bell pepper- 1
- Diced onion- 1
- Diced tomatoes- 8
- Italian seasoning- 1 tbsp.
- Crushed red pepper flakes- 1 tsp.

―――――――――――――――――――――――――――――

Preparation:

Preheat your oven to 350 degrees Fahrenheit.

Stuff the chicken with the Italian sausages.

Put the diced green pepper, diced onion and diced tomatoes around the chicken thighs.

Season the chicken thighs with Italian seasoning and crushed red pepper flakes.

Bake the prepared chicken in the preheated oven for 35 to 40 minutes or until the chicken is done.

Serve!

Noodle Napoli

This is an Italian noodle dish served in winter.

Duration: 10 minutes.

Serving Size: 5.

List of Ingredients:

- Ground beef- 1 pound
- Italian sausage- ½ pound
- Oil- 2 tbsp.
- Onion- 1
- Garlic clove- 1
- Egg noodles- 8 ounces
- Pimento peppers- 4 ounces
- Blended tomatoes- 8 ounces
- Water- 2 cups
- Shredded cheddar cheese- 1 cup

Preparation:

Heat water in a large pan and boil in the egg noodles.

Drain and set aside.

Heat oil in a saucepan and fry in the onion, garlic clove, ground beef and Italian sausage.

Now add in the diced pimento pepper and the blended tomatoes.

Simmer to let the beef cook.

Stir in the cheddar cheese.

Now mix in the cooked egg noodles.

Serve!

Sausage Cheese Balls

These cheese balls are made with either chicken sausage or lamb meat. They are very delicious in taste and are mostly served at Christmas parties.

Duration: 20 minutes.

Serving Size: 24.

List of Ingredients:

- Lamb sausage- 1 pound
- Butter milk mix- 1 ½ cups
- Shredded cheddar cheese- 4 cups
- Chopped onion- ½
- Garlic powder or crushed garlic- ½ tsp.
- Celery stalk- 1

||||||||||||||||||||||||||||||||||||||||||||||||||||||||||||||||||||||||||||||

Preparation:

It is up to you, your choice, whether you want to bake these cheese balls or want to fry them. In both cases, the taste is the same amazing one and the cheese balls turn out to be very crispy.

Mix the sausages, butter milk mix, cheddar cheese, green onion and celery.

Season with the garlic powder.

Form into balls and bake at 375 degrees Fahrenheit or fry them.

Broccoli, Rabe and Sausage

This is a quick and simple recipe that is healthy as well.

Duration: 15 minutes

Serving Size: 8

List of Ingredients:

- Broccoli rabe- 1
- Salt- 1 tbsp.
- Olive oil- 6 tbsp.
- Sausage- 1 pound
- Garlic cloves- 2
- Lemon juice- ¼ cup

Preparation:

Boil the broccoli rabe with salted water in a large pot until soft.

Heat olive oil in a pan and fry in the sausage.

Remove from heat and mix in the garlic and the lemon juice.

Mix in the broccoli rabe with the remaining liquid and simmer for a few minutes before serving.

Sausage, Kale and White Bean Soup

This is a delicious soup on a cold winter day.

Duration: 15 minutes

Serving Size: 8

List of Ingredients:

- Beans- 1 cup
- Kale- a bunch
- Olive oil- 1 tbsp.
- Sausage- 1 pound
- Chopped shallots- 1 cup
- Chicken broth- 4 cups
- Salt- a pinch
- Pepper- a pinch
- Hot sauce- ½ tsp.

Preparation:

Soak the beans in water overnight and then cook them in a pressure cooker the next day.

Cook the kale in salted water, drain and set aside.

Fry the sausage in a pan.

Then fry in the shallots and add in the chicken broth.

Now mix the sausage in the kale, shallots and chicken broth.

Mix in the beans.

Season with salt and pepper.

Simmer for a few minutes.

Add in the hot sauce and then serve!

Burrata Stuffed Burger

In this burger, burrata cheese is used which has a great taste. Moreover, the fish sauce gives a unique taste to the patty. If you want a low carb burger recipe, the only thing which you need to do is to skip the bun.

Duration: 30 minutes.

Serving Size: 2.

List of Ingredients:

- Ground beef sausage- 1 pound
- Fish sauce- 1 ½ tsp.
- Salt- 1 tsp.
- Black pepper- ½ tbsp.
- Burrata cheese- 8 ounces
- Bacon slices- 6
- Spinach leaves- a few

Preparation:

In a bowl, add the beef sausage, bacon slices, fish sauce, salt and pepper and mix properly.

Form patties.

Place one slice of burrata on each patty and then one more patty on the burrata cheese slice.

After resting the burgers for a few minutes, heat up your griller and season your patties with salt and pepper.

Grill them on each side for a few minutes until they are cooked properly.

Serve!

German Currywurst

Currywurst is a kind of German fast food which is very popular in Berlin. It is very quick and easy to make, and you can use ketchup as a seasoning or serve it with any kind of sauce you want.

Duration: 10 minutes.

Serving Size: 4.

List of Ingredients:

- Tomato sauce- 45 ounces
- Chili sauce- 2 tbsp.
- Kielbasa sausage- 1 pound
- Sugar- 1 tbsp.
- Onion salt- ½ tsp.
- Ground black pepper- 1 tsp.
- Paprika- a pinch
- Curry powder- a pinch

Preparation:

Add the tomato sauce into a large saucepan.

Add in the onion salt, chili sauce, sugar and black pepper.

Bring to boil and then let simmer for a few minutes.

Grill the kielbasa sausage in your oven broiler for 4 minutes on each side and dish out.

Pour over the tomato sauce mixtures on the broiled sausage.

Serve!

Beer Brats

These are amazing beer brats that are first broiled and then grilled.

Duration: 5 minutes

Serving Size: 10

List of Ingredients:

- Beer- 48 ounces
- Onion- 1
- Bratwurst- 10
- Red pepper flakes- 2 tsp.
- Garlic powder- 1 tsp.
- Salt- 1 tsp.
- Black pepper- ½ tsp.

Preparation:

Take a large pot and mix in the beer and the onion.

Now mix in the bratwurst.

Now add in the red pepper flakes and the garlic powder.

Season with salt and black pepper.

Remove the bratwurst from the mixture and grill them on a preheated griller for a few minutes.

Serve with the beer mixture!

Sausage Barley Soup

This is a very nice soup recipe with a lot of flavor and texture.

Duration: 15 minutes

Serving Size: 4

List of Ingredients:

- Italian sausage- 1 pound
- Onion- ½
- Garlic- 1 tbsp.
- Italian seasoning- ½ tsp.
- Chicken broth- 48 ounces
- Carrot- 1
- Chopped spinach- 10 ounces
- Barley- ¼ cup

Preparation:

Fry the Italian sausage, onion and garlic.

Season it with the Italian seasoning and then remove from heat.

Take a slow cooker and add in the Italian sausage mixture and mix in the chicken broth, carrot, chopped spinach and barley.

Cook on low heat for 3 to 4 hours.

Serve!

Jalapeno and Blue Cheese Burger

The jalapeno gives a real kick to this burger, and the crumbled blue cheese gives a very gooey flavor to it.

Duration: 10 minutes.

Serving Size: 1.

List of Ingredients:

- Sausage- 100 grams
- Garlic clove- 1
- Jalapeno- ½
- Salt- a pinch
- Pepper- a pinch
- Paprika- ½ tsp.
- Tomato- ½
- Lettuce - 1
- Blue cheese- 3 tbsp.

Preparation:

In a bowl, mix the meat, crushed garlic, jalapeno, salt, pepper, blue cheese and paprika.

Mix properly and make patties from the meat.

Grill the patties until cooked.

Top the patties with slices of tomato and wrap the patty with the lettuce leaf and serve.

Toscana Soup

This is a creamy and delicious soup with some healthy vegetables!

Duration: 10 minutes.

Serving Size: 5.

List of Ingredients:

- Sausages- 12
- Oil- 1 tbsp.
- Diced onion- ¾ cup
- Garlic- 1 tsp.
- Chicken soup base- 2 tbsp.
- Water- 4 cups
- Potatoes- 2
- Sliced kale- 2 cups
- Cream- 1/3 cup

Preparation:

Bake your sausages in the oven at 300 degrees Fahrenheit until browned.

Chop them.

Add oil in a pot and add in the baked sausages and the onion.

Fry for a few minutes and add in the garlic and the soup base.

Add in the water and the potatoes and cook till they are tender.

Now add in the sliced kale and let it simmer.

Finally, add in the cream and then serve.

Italian Style Nachos

Try this new version of making nachos with an Italian touch to it!

Duration: 15 minutes.

Serving Size: 8.

List of Ingredients:

- Italian sausage- 1 pound
- Tortilla chips- 8 ounces
- Sliced pepperoni- 2 ounces
- Shredded mozzarella cheese- ½ pound
- Banana peppers- ½ cup
- Pizza sauce- 1 ¼ cups

Preparation:

Preheat the broiler of your oven.

Cook the Italian sausage in the skillet.

Arrange the tortilla chips on a baking tray.

Top with the cooked Italian sausage, sliced pepperoni, shredded mozzarella cheese and banana peppers.

Put in the oven for a few minutes or until the cheese has melted.

Serve with the pizza sauce as a dip.

German Spaghetti

This dish is made with juicy and flavorful beef, sausage, tomato sauce and bacon.

Duration: 1 hour 5 minutes

Serving Size: 8.

List of Ingredients:

- Grounded beef- 1 pound
- Italian sausage- ¼ cup
- Bacon slices- 6
- Tomato sauce- 15 ounces
- Canned tomatoes- 28 ounces
- Sugar- 1/3 cup
- Spaghetti- 12 ounces
- Oil- 2 tbsp.

Preparation:

Boil the spaghetti in a large saucepan filled with water.

Drain and set aside.

Add oil in a frying pan and fry the ground beef until it is cooked.

Remove from heat and now fry the sausage in the frying pan.

Now add in the cooked beef.

Add in the bacon slices, tomato sauce, tomatoes and canned tomatoes.

Let it simmer for 40 to 45 minutes.

Now mix the cooked spaghetti in the tomato mixture.

Pour this in a baking rectangular dish.

Preheat your oven to 300 degrees Fahrenheit.

Put this baking dish in the preheated oven to bake for 30 minutes.

Serve!

Divine Burger

This burger is so easy to make, but at the same time, it is actually delicious in taste. The ingredients are quite simple, and it is a low carb burger.

Duration: 10 minutes.

Serving Size: 7

List of Ingredients:

- Sausage - 16 ounces
- Pepper and onion - 12 ounces
- Low carb thickener - ¾ tsp.
- Garlic powder - ½ tsp.
- Salt - ½ tsp.
- Pepper - ¼ tsp.
- Italian seasoning - 4 tbsp.

Preparation:

In a bowl, add the Italian sausages, garlic powder, salt, pepper and low carb thickener and mix.

Put this mixture in a pan to cook.

Cut the pepper and onion and add to the pan to cook.

Once cooked, dish out the mixture.

Form patties when the mixture is cooled.

Grill these patties on a griller or fry them in a pan.

Drizzle Italian seasoning on top of each patty and serve!

Pork and Pepper Stir Fry

This is a very easy and spicy stir fry recipe. If you do not wish to make the dish with pork, you can substitute it with chicken or meat also.

Duration: 1 hour 10 minutes.

Serving Size: 4.

List of Ingredients:

- Rice wine vinegar- ¼ cup
- Minced garlic- 2 tbsp.
- Brown sugar- 1 tbsp.
- Olive oil- 5 tbsp.
- Salt- a pinch
- Pepper- a pinch
- Pork sausages- 4
- Vegetable oil- 5 tbsp.
- Ginger root- 3 tbsp.
- Chile paste- 1 tbsp.
- Teriyaki sauce- 5 tbsp.
- Green pepper- 1
- Red pepper- 1
- Yellow pepper- 1
- Salt and pepper- a pinch
- Blanched almonds- ¼ cup
- Chopped mint- 2 tbsp.

Preparation:

Chop the pork sausages and marinate them with rice wine vinegar, minced garlic, brown sugar, olive oil, salt and pepper.

Coat properly.

Toast the almonds in a wok until they turn golden brown.

Heat vegetable oil in a pan and stir fry the marinated sausages in the pan.

Add the ginger and the chili paste.

Now add the teriyaki sauce and cook on high heat for a few minutes.

Now add in the red pepper, green pepper and yellow pepper and fry.

Cook until the pork turns white in color.

Garnish with sliced and toasted almonds and chopped mint leaves.

Serve!

Low Carb Cheddar Cheese and Beef Burger

The flavor of cheddar cheese makes this burger so delicious and cheesy. The recipe is a low carb and gluten free burger.

Duration: 15 minutes

Serving Size: 2.

List of Ingredients:

- Italian sausage- ¼ lb.
- Salt- ½ tsp.
- Black pepper- ½ tsp.
- Mustard- 12 tsp.
- Lettuce leaves- 4
- Tomato slices- 2
- Onion slices- 2
- Cheddar cheese slices- 2

Preparation:

Add salt and pepper to the sausages and form patties.

Cook or grill the patties until done.

Spread mustard on each patty and top it with tomato slices, onion slices and cheddar cheese slices.

Top with another patty and wrap lettuce leaves around the patty.

Serve!

German Style Kale and Sausage

This is a German style dish belonging to the northern areas of Germany where the severity of cold makes the dish worth eating.

Duration: 20 minutes.

Serving Size: 4.

List of Ingredients:

- Chopped kale- 1 pound
- Bacon slices- 3
- Chopped onion- ½
- Water- 2 cups
- Beef bouillon cubes- 2 tsp.
- Ground nutmeg- ¼ tsp.
- Mustard- 1 tbsp.
- Cooked ham- ½ pound
- Kielbasa sausages- 2
- Salt- a pinch
- Pepper- a pinch
- Oil- 2 tbsp.

Preparation:

Add 1 cup of water and blanch in the kale.

Add oil in a skillet and fry the chopped onion.

Mix in the kale, beef bouillon cubes, nutmeg, mustard, ham, sausage, salt and pepper.

Add the remaining water and let it simmer for about 35 minutes or until everything is cooked to perfection.

Serve!

Breakfast Sausage

This is a homemade breakfast sausage recipe that you can make from ground pork and spices.

Duration: 10 minutes

Serving Size: 6

List of Ingredients:

- Sage- 2 tsp.
- Salt- 2 tsp.
- Black pepper- 1 tsp.
- Marjoram- ¼ tsp.
- Brown sugar- 1 tbsp.
- Red pepper flakes- 1/8 tsp.
- Cloves- a pinch
- Ground pork- 2 pounds

Preparation:

Mix together the sage, salt, black pepper, marjoram, brown sugar, red pepper flakes and cloves.

Mix in the ground pork and then form patties.

Grill the patties on each side until cooked well.

Serve!

Low Carb Blue Cheese Burger

The recipe is so amazing that you will forget other recipes. Marinated beef along with portobello mushrooms and blue cheese is the perfect yummy burger.

Duration: 10 minutes.

Serving Size: 3

List of Ingredients:

- Italian sausages- 1 pound
- Worcestershire sauce- 1 tbsp.
- Steak seasoning- 1 tbsp.
- Blue cheese- 4 ounces
- Portobello mushrooms- 3
- Onion slices - 4
- Salad dressing- ¼ cup
- Butter- 1 ounce
- Blue cheese- 2 ounces
- Parsley- 1 tbsp.
- Shallots- 2 tsp.

Preparation:

Mix the parsley and the shallots.

Add the butter and mash with a fork.

Add the blue cheese.

Mix and roll the mixture into log shapes on waxed paper and refrigerate.

Cut the onion into rings.

Clean the mushrooms.

Mix the mushrooms and the onion rings in the salad dressing.

Grill the Portobello mushrooms and cook the onions.

Add the steak seasoning and the Worcestershire sauce in the beef and the blue cheese and mix.

Make patties and grill them.

Place the grilled patties on the mushrooms and then put the butter mixture and top it with the onions.

Sprinkle parsley and serve with fried shallots.

Sausage and Red Cabbage

This dish can be served with mashed potatoes and mustard pickles.

Duration: 30 minutes.

Serving Size: 5.

List of Ingredients:

- Shredded cabbage head - 1
- Apple- 1
- Salt- 3 tsp.
- Lemon juice- 1 tbsp.
- Water- ½ cup
- Butter- 1 tbsp.
- Onion- 1
- Black pepper- 1/8 tsp.
- Wine vinegar- 1 tbsp.
- Sausage- 1 pound

Preparation:

In a saucepan, add the shredded cabbage, apple, 2 tsp. of salt, lemon juice and water.

Bring it to a boil and then simmer to let the cabbage cook.

In another pan, heat the butter and fry the onions.

Stir the onion in the cabbage.

Now add the rest of the salt, pepper, vinegar and sausage.

Cook and cover.

Serve!

Cilantro and Pork Sausage

Topped with cilantro, this pork sausage dish is a delicious recipe. With little preparation and cooking time, this is a very simple and very easy to make one as well.

Duration: 15 minutes.

Serving Size: 4.

List of Ingredients:

- Olive oil- ¼ cup
- Chopped cilantro leaves- ½ cup
- Chopped ginger- 1 tbsp.
- Chopped garlic cloves - 4
- Sliced pork sausage- 1 pound
- Olive oil- 2 tbsp.
- Sliced onions- 2
- Red pepper- 1
- Lemon juice- 1 tbsp.
- Chopped fresh cilantro- ½ cup

Preparation:

Mix the olive oil, ½ cup cilantro, ginger and garlic.

Mix in the sliced pork pieces to coat evenly.

Marinate for a while or more if you have time to marinate for the night.

Heat oil in a wok and stir fry the pork pieces until they are cooked properly.

Set aside the pork pieces.

Fry the onions for a few minutes, then add the peppers and fry them.

Add in the fried pork.

Now add the lemon juice and the chopped cilantro.

Cook for a minute and then serve!

Pork and Sausage Fried Rice

This pork and sausage fried rice is made with a variety of vegetables and can be served with a nice gravy or something else it could be eaten just like that. The combination of the vegetables gives the rice a good taste.

Duration: 30 minutes.

Serving Size: 2.

List of Ingredients:

- Butter- 1 tbsp.
- Pork sausage- 6 ounces
- Chopped broccoli- ¼ cup
- Chopped carrot- ¼ cup
- Green onion- 1
- Egg- 1
- Frozen peas- ¼ cup
- Cold cooked rice- 1 cup
- Soya sauce- 1 ½ tbsp.
- Garlic powder- 1/8 tsp.
- Ground ginger- 1/8 tsp.

Preparation:

Melt the butter in a pot and add in the pork sausages and fry.

Add in the chopped carrot and chopped broccoli.

Now add in the frozen peas and the green onions.

Cook until the pork is cooked.

Remove the cooked pork and set aside.

Beat the egg and scramble it in the same pot.

Add in the pork mixture.

Now add in the cooked rice, frozen peas, soya sauce, garlic powder and ground ginger and stir until everything is mixed in properly.

Cook for a few minutes.

Serve!

Portobello Mushroom and Pizza Burger

This is a unique recipe for a low carb burger made with sauce and pepperoni slices. Italian sausages are also added to the burger.

Duration: 15 minutes.

Serving Size: 4.

List of Ingredients:

- Portobello mushrooms- 4
- Italian sausage- 1 pound
- Mozzarella cheese slices- 8
- Pepperoni slices- 20
- Cherry tomatoes- 3
- Salt- 1 tsp.
- Basil- for garnishing

llllllllllllllllllllllllllllllllllllllllllllllllllllllllllllllllllllllllllllllllllllllll

Preparation:

Clean the mushrooms

Form patties from the Italian sausage.

Grill the mushrooms on the griller.

Make the sauce by blending the cherry tomatoes and the salt.

Spoon a little bit of sauce on each mushroom.

Cook the sausage patties and the mushrooms.

Place pepperoni slices and mozzarella slices on each patty until the cheese is melted.

Remove from heat and serve on a plate and garnish with basil and more sauce.

Country Sausage Gravy

This is an excellent sausage recipe that you can use for your breakfast!

Duration: 15 minutes

Serving Size: 4

List of Ingredients:

- Sausage- 1 pound
- Onion- 1
- Green bell pepper- 1
- Red pepper flakes- 1 tsp.
- Garlic- 2 tbsp.
- Butter- 4 tbsp.
- Salt- a pinch
- Pepper- a pinch
- Flour- 4 tbsp.
- Sage- 1 tsp.
- Thyme- 1 tsp.
- Milk- 2 cups
- Chicken bouillon cubes - 2
- Parsley- ¼ cup

Preparation:

In a skillet, fry the pork sausage, onion, green bell pepper, red pepper flakes and garlic.

Now mix in the butter, salt and pepper.

Mix the flour gently and then the sage and thyme.

Now add in the milk gradually as required.

Put in the chicken bouillon cubes.

Simmer for a while before serving.

Sprinkle over with parsley.

Boere Breyani

This biryani is a traditional South African recipe full of flavor.

Duration: 15 minutes.

Serving Size: 6.

List of Ingredients:

- Boerewors- ½ kg
- Chutney- 1.5 cups
- Turmeric- 1 tsp.
- Curry powder- 4 tbsp.
- Green pepper-1
- Onions-3
- Brown lentils- ½ cup
- Rice- 2 cups
- Salt and pepper- 1 tsp.
- Water – 1 cup
- Apricot slices- 825 g

Preparation:

Cut the boerewors and put them in a dish. Place the apricots on them.

Add salt and pepper, rice and brown lentils.

In another pan, fry the onions in oil, add the green pepper. Add the turmeric, chutney, curry powder and water.

Mix and pour over the boerewors mixture.

Cover it and bake in the oven for 45 minutes at 180 degrees Fahrenheit until all the liquid is absorbed.

Tuscan Soup

This is a spicy Tuscan soup with potatoes, spinach and sausage.

Duration: 20 minutes.

Serving Size: 4.

List of Ingredients:

- Chicken broth- 6 cups
- Chopped onion- 1
- Italian sausage- 9 ounces
- Potatoes- 3
- Spinach- a bunch
- Evaporated milk- ¼ cup
- Salt- a pinch
- Black pepper- a pinch

Preparation:

Crumble the sausages and fry them in a frying pan.

Now add in the chopped onion and cook for a few minutes.

Transfer to a large pot and add in the potatoes and the chicken broth.

Add in the spinach and cook until the potatoes are cooked.

Remove from heat and then add in the evaporated milk, salt and pepper.

Serve!

Italian Sausage Soup

This is an extremely healthy soup that works wonders in winter!

Duration: 10 minutes

Serving Size: 6

List of Ingredients:

- Italian sausage- 1 pound
- Garlic clove- 1
- Beef broth- 28 ounces
- Tomatoes- 15 ounces
- Sliced carrots- 1 cup
- Beans- 15 ounces
- Zucchini- 1
- Spinach- 2 cups
- Black pepper- ¼ tsp.
- Salt- ¼ tsp.

Preparation:

Take a saucepan and add in the Italian sausage and the garlic.

Fry for a few minutes.

Then add in the beef broth, tomatoes, sliced carrots, beans, zucchini and spinach.

Simmer the mixture for an hour or until the vegetables are cooked properly.

Season with salt and pepper.

Pour into bowls and serve!

BBQ Nachos

Make these barbeque nachos for a quick and light snack for your afternoon treat.

Duration: 5 minutes.

Serving Size: 2.

List of Ingredients:

- Tortilla chips- 20
- Smoked beef sausage- ¼ pound
- Cheddar cheese- ½ cup
- Barbeque sauce- ¼ cup

Preparation:

Preheat your oven to 350 degrees Fahrenheit.

Spread the nachos in a baking tray.

Top the nachos with the smoked beef sausage and the cheddar cheese.

Put the nachos to bake in the preheated oven for 15 to 20 minutes or until the cheese has melted properly.

Drizzle over the barbeque sauce and then serve!

You can alternatively microwave the nachos until the cheese melts and then serve with the barbeque sauce!

Biography

For decades, this beautiful actress graced our screens with her incredible talent and performance in movies that captivated the script and emotions of the viewers. Well, life rarely goes as planned, but we should always make the best out of it, like Chloe.

Originally from the bubbly city of Los Angeles, she has moved from the movie industry into the food scene. Her role in Mama Mia ignited her passion for food. She has taken the New York scene by surprise. Charmed by the unique regions she had visited, the delicious delicacies she tasted, her uncanny appreciation for flavors, ingredients, and cooking techniques have continued to wow customers wide and far.

However, as mentioned, she started as an actress. Breaking into the food scene was easy because she had contacts and connections, but satisfying clients was a different ball game. Over the years, she has mastered the food scenes and unique flavors clients seek. Today, her clients can attest to the high-quality food from her restaurants.

The New York food scene is a jungle that only the strong dare to tread. However, she was a passionate student and learned the tricks and tips, and slowly set her passion for delivering excellent tastes to all who sought them.

An Author's Afterthought

Did you like my book? I pondered it severely before releasing this book. Although the response has been overwhelming, it is always pleasing to see, read or hear a new comment. Thank you for reading this and I would love to hear your honest opinion about it. Furthermore, many people are searching for a unique book, and your feedback will help me gather the right books for my reading audience.

Thanks!

Chloe Tucker

Printed in Great Britain
by Amazon